The Agony and Ecstasy of the Landlord

Natasha Re

LifeRich Publishing is a registered trademark of
The Reader's Digest Association, Inc.

This book is a work of non-fiction. Unless otherwise noted, the author
and the publisher make no explicit guarantees as to the accuracy of
the information contained in this book and in some cases, names of
people and places have been altered to protect their privacy.

LifeRich Publishing books may be ordered through booksellers or by contacting:

LifeRich Publishing
1663 Liberty Drive
Bloomington, IN 47403
www.liferichpublishing.com
1 (888) 238-8637

Because of the dynamic nature of the Internet, any web addresses or
links contained in this book may have changed since publication and
may no longer be valid. The views expressed in this work are solely those
of the author and do not necessarily reflect the views of the publisher,
and the publisher hereby disclaims any responsibility for them.

Any people depicted in stock imagery provided by Getty Images are
models, and such images are being used for illustrative purposes only.
Certain stock imagery © Getty Images.

ISBN: 978-1-4897-2066-5 (sc)
ISBN: 978-1-4897-2067-2 (e)

Library of Congress Control Number: 2018966225

Print information available on the last page.

LifeRich Publishing rev. date: 12/31/2018

CONTENTS

Introduction.. xi

The Properties from Hell 1
The Remodel.. 9
Tenants, Problems and Solutions 15
The Agony and Ecstasy of the Landlord................ 23
Income, Expenses and More 49
Saving Grace 57
The Inevitable 63

Recommended Readings 65
About the Author... 67

This book is dedicated to all those who dream big and never stop trying.

INTRODUCTION

I want to share my landlord and real estate investor experiences in the hopes to enlighten someone about some of the obstacles and unexpected situations in the real estate world of investing just the way I experienced it.

Background

Real estate has been a passion of mine since I was young. I wanted to grow up to be a construction worker but in those days that was only a man's job. Our neighbor Mr. Sanchez was the family's lifetime contractor and every opportunity I got to watch him work I was there. The smell of cement mixing and moist dirt always bring me back to those days.

As soon as I had my first job at age 18 I started to look for a home to buy, no I did not make enough money to qualify or had the credit scores required but I figured I would gather all my brothers and sisters and convince them to invest with me and at age 19 I purchased my first home with the help of almost all my siblings, making that my most successful investment.

When my husband and I got married we owned 3 properties, made a good living, we had great paying jobs and spent it all. We felt entitled to spend all the money we earned and as soon as we thought of another purchase of any kind, it was done! I used to worry about our spending and figured that by buying real estate it would force us to save since we were not disciplined enough to save in any other way. It was definitely not the way to go at least not when we were borrowing the money to buy or invest.

I always felt rushed to look for investment properties and hoped to acquire as many as possible before we would spend the money somewhere else, believing that would be our saving grace for retirement. I kept remembering the quote by Carnegie;

"90% of all millionaires become so through owning real estate." – Andrew Carnegie

But everything changes when the unexpected happens; job loss, bad economy, and bills piling up and for me there comes the properties from hell. A lesson learned and worth sharing.

Some names and identifying details have been changed to protect the privacy of individuals. Any resemblance to actual persons, living or dead, or actual events is purely coincidental.

THE PROPERTIES FROM HELL

It all began in 2003 when I saw an advertisement in a Spanish Newspaper about 3 properties being sold by owner. They were $40k each with only $5k down payment. Hard to find properties anywhere in the states for this price, and the terms to obtain them was too good to be true but it was real! They offered them with an amortized private loan for 25 years at 10.5% interest rate. There were two loans, one for $40k and another one for $75k.

There were two separate adjoining lots, one a duplex and one a single-family residence. The three properties complimented each other because they all covered a corner lot. Since the sale was directly from the owner, there was no real estate agent involved, and therefore, not paying a commission fee was attractive in itself, an immediate bonus!

When I drove up to see them I loved the long peaceful drive with mountain views, grape vines, orange and lemon trees and even in some parts there was no cell phone signal, a town where everyone knew each other. It reminded me of the town where I grew up.

When I saw the properties I fell in love with them. The houses were built in 1929, they were small, had character and a decent size lot.

The houses had solid bones, had just be renovated but needed some final minor cosmetic fixes such as wood floor refinishing, a couple of cracked windows, bathrooms touch ups, some fresh paint, the kitchen cabinets of one property had to be refinished and the landscaping could use some new plants or grass and maybe fences to separate the properties and give tenants some privacy. It did not scare me, I had a handyman that I used for my other properties and I knew he would fix them up in no time.

There was an enormous pomegranate bush full of fruit and two gigantic mature trees, each one providing shade to the units in the duplex.

The duplex did not have any garages but there was a long driveway in between. There was an alley too and parking in front and to the side street as well. The back unit was a two-story building and the living area was above two garages. The tenants from the duplex were using one garage each. That was the reason why selling the 3 units made sense.

The back unit had its own detached garage and in the middle of them was a gazebo. I imagined these properties being like the tenants own little community where they would have a private area to socialize.

The seller Mr. Gomez, commented that most of the tenants were Spanish speaking coming from the surrounding farming areas and mentioned that if I spoke Spanish I would have no problem renting the units right away and the seller's sister Martha offered to be the property manager for a 6% fee instead of the typical 10% fee that other property managers charged. I just could not think of a reason why NOT to buy them! I did my calculations and figured the rents would cover the monthly payments, taxes and insurance and what a better way to assist the low-income farmer communities and make a difference!

I saw so much potential and even imagined ourselves living there, a total change of pace from where we lived but in case the economy would crash and we lose our nice paying jobs and other investments this could be our back up plan. Losing our jobs was always a worry in the back of my mind and hoped we could rely in our investments to float and continue to build our wealth in one way or another.

My husband was not too crazy about these properties because of the distance and the small town feel, he preferred to stay close to the city.

I was determined and I asked my sister to join me in the venture. She was interested but wanted to do it by herself. I then figured if she was willing to do it by herself then I should be able to do it by myself. I convinced my husband and offered to buy them under my name only just in case of anything going wrong. He was still not too happy about it but just went along with it.

I negotiated with the private investor Mr. Reitz for a lower interest rate of 9% and no prepayment penalty, due to my excellent credit rating. I was confident I could pay them off quickly, the amounts were so small I could even charge them, a few of my credit cards had credit limits of over $40k with no balances and I was counting on a couple of decent commissions from my job which might, just might pay off at least one of the loans if not both, no worries!

Mr. Reitz set up an appointment with the escrow company to close the deal and I handed out the deposit check of $5,000.00, which was a check from Chase of 0% interest rate for one year. I had many of those checks coming in every month from Chase, Bank of America, Capital One, Wells Fargo, etc.

I decided to hire Martha to be the property manager since she was familiar with the process, the people, the town and she lived blocks away from the properties.

It was an exciting time, I was going to provide affordable and newly remodeled housing to low-income families and I was the owner of a multifamily property; I was on my way to build our family's empire!

THE REMODEL

As soon as escrow closed, Martha the property manager called me to tell me that she was not going to be able to manage the properties because her daughter who lived 80 miles away had been in a terrible car accident and was not able to care for her small children. Martha was to move with her daughter for an indefinite period of time, possibly a permanent move.

I worried but thought it would not be a problem, I could handle it I had plenty of experience in property management, the only challenge was the distance, these properties were 103 miles away from my primary residence.

I immediately started the renovation so I could rent the units right away. When I called my handyman Mr. Palacios to tell him what I had done, he said he was willing to drive up with me to see the properties but thought it might be too far from him to do the job. He lived almost 200 miles away, one way, but was still interested in considering the project. I picked him up and we drove up together.

We went around town and found only one hardware store with limited building materials at a much higher price than the big stores such as Home Depot or Lowes, the closest Home Depot and Lowes were 20 miles away which did not seem too bad to me. Mr. Palacios said he would do the job, but only by staying in a local hotel for the week and it would take about two months to finish. I immediately saw the remodeling numbers going up very fast. I told him I was going to find out about the local workers or construction companies to see if I could economize a bit. I was planning of using one of my credit cards with the $40k credit limit for the renovations and was hoping to spend as little as possible to leave room for emergencies.

I found out that there were not many local construction companies or handymen willing to take my small job. The local ones would not drive to the nearest town where the Home Depot and Lowes were to purchase the materials needed and the outsider contractors were not willing to drive to where the properties were. Neither wanted to travel 20 miles back and forth as needed. By this time Mr. Palacios was not interested in taking the job, he had started a big project that would take several months.

Mr. Gomez, the seller, was not returning my calls about asking them for referrals. The only referral company they gave me was the home insurance company and after that they disappeared completely. I also found out that not all insurance companies would insure properties that old and if they did then the premiums were much higher and were stricter with the coverage.

I decided to do one thing at a time, the most urgent ones such as fixing the broken windows first and I hired the local glass company. They were more expensive than the big town shops but I needed it done so I had to pay the high price. Then I found out that the windows had different dimensions because these were old style windows and nobody had them in stock, which was part of the charm of the house. The new ready and available windows were not the kind I needed so my windows had to be ordered and of course more expensive because they were custom made.

No problem, I had plenty of credit in my credit cards to cover that and more so the windows were ordered.

After about 2 or 3 weeks of ownership I was still not able to find a reliable handyman or construction worker, the referrals I got were not responding to my calls.

I reluctantly called my 19 year old nephew to ask him if he had a friend or knew of someone interested in finishing up these properties and if they would be able to stay in the houses while fixing them, they lived over 70 miles away. He was enthusiastic and said this would be an adventure for them. He recruited two other friends who had construction experience. My nephew only knew how to build fences but his friends could do the rest. We decided the houses needed to be fenced because they were in a corner lot and the fence would protect them in case of an accident or simply to provide more privacy.

I was excited about it and when we met at the houses we found out there were roaches, ants and other types of bugs, we needed to fumigate the houses if they were to stay there. Because I wanted it done quickly I offered to pay for them to stay in one of the local motels for as long as needed.

The remodeling was complete in about 4 weeks, including the fences. Some things were still missing but the places were ready to be rented. This took many more trips from me, food and hotel expenses for all but no problem I thought, I had plenty of credit in my credit card and a paycheck too.

TENANTS, PROBLEMS AND SOLUTIONS

I began to advertise in the local paper, posted signs at the local Laundromats, markets and signs outside of the houses. I advertised in English and Spanish and was ready to be bombarded with calls and excited to meet prospect tenants. Sure enough the calls came!

I started setting appointments to show the houses and fill out applications, most applicants did not have any electronic way of communication such as e-mail or fax. I scheduled various prospects at the same time because I knew some of them would not be showing up and it was just not easy to go back and forth to show one tenant at a time. Every time I went back to meet with prospect tenants the signs outside of the house were missing so I put new signs inside the house windows, which were hard to see from the street but at least they stayed there.

I had a few open houses and people would pick up the applications but did not return them. Sometimes as soon as I would return home I would receive a call from someone wanting to see the inside of the houses at that time and of course I was not able to show it because I was miles and miles away so I don't know if those were serious tenants or not, the opportunity was gone.

Finally after many trips, many shows and many no shows I found a great young family for one house Mr. and Mrs. Flores with their 2 daughters, another couple, Mr. and Mrs. Otto for another house and a single young male, Mr. Hazan, for the other. Surprisingly enough, not very many Spanish-speaking low-income families from the farming community applied which was a bit disappointing since that was one of the main reasons I wanted to buy these properties but at least one of the leases was for one of them and all these tenants seemed to be pleased to have a place to call home.

All the applicants had decent credit and great references but all had limited income, which was not a surprise due to the lack of local job opportunities. The people with better incomes owned their homes, the real estate prices were reasonable.

My favorite tenants were Mr. and Mrs. Flores they signed a 5-year lease contract. They loved the house it was perfect for them, one room for them and one for the little girls, it was fenced so the kids could play safely outside, they were anxious to do landscaping work, plant flowers and make this place their home. They were the Hispanics who worked in the local farming fields. They did not have much to show of furniture or other material belongings or even a checking account and they didn't have enough for the security deposit so they asked if it was possible to pay it in 4 months because they had some money coming in at that time. I went ahead and agreed to it, I figured they were going to be there for a long time, why not?

Every time I picked up the rent from them on the first of the month the rent money came in cash and with a box of fresh delicious chili peppers and/or tomatoes from where they were farming.

They maintained the yard and the house clean, or maybe it just looked clean because there was almost no furniture anywhere. I was planning on gathering household goods and just stuff from my house that I was not using to give to them. I assumed their salary was low and didn't have much to splurge on household decorations and I had so much I could do without. Boy, this was just the kind of goodwill I wanted to be a part of and these properties were giving me the opportunity to do so!

The other tenants Mr. and Mrs. Otto, were a young couple in their early 20's who were trying to start a family. He was a truck driver and she was planning to be a stay home mom, she was trying to get pregnant and was hoping to work from home sometime after having the baby. She loved to read, was computer literate and thought she might work from home doing something related to computers and contribute to the household expenses as soon as they would settle in.

Most of their belongings were books, which I thought was a good sign. Because there was only one steady income I gave them a discount with the rent and they signed a one-year lease.

Mr. Hazan, the single male tenant worked at the local supermarket where he could walk to and from the house, it was so close he was able to go home for lunch. He wanted a month-to-month lease because he was more comfortable that way. I agreed to it even though I was looking for long term tenants, he was being honest about the commitment he was willing to make and I assumed with his job so close he would be there for a long time, he assured me he had no plans to go anywhere and since I did not have any other prospects I signed him up.

After renting the units I continued to look for a local handyman that would be able to work with me on a regular basis for maintenance on the properties with not much success.

As I was balancing out my bills and the rents deposits I realized I had not received the bill from the credit card I used for the $5,000.00 check I wrote for the deposit of the houses. I assumed it cleared since the private lender had not mentioned anything and I had already made my first two loan payments but I was too busy to even notice the credit card bill missing. I called the credit company and they said the bill had been returned. It was mailed to my P.O. Box that I had for a few years. I was surprised to hear that and asked for the bill to confirm that it had indeed been returned so I could find out what happened at the post office. Few days passed and sure enough I received the returned bill along with the new statement showing a late fee of $65.00 AND a new term; A balance of $5,000.00 at a 29% interest rate!

The rate had changed from 0% to 29%. In the small print it said that any payment defaults would revert back the rate to the maximum rate allowed of 29%. I called and explained what happened but the credit card company would not make any changes to the interest rate, they would only wave the $65.00 fee. There was nothing else to do other than to pay it off as soon as possible, the monthly payment increased tremendously.

As soon as the interests went down I refinanced the duplex. It was appraised 3 times more than the purchase price which was much more than I had expected and the lending company offered me a 65% maximum loan amount at 6.25% interest rate. It was a very tempting offer for an investment property but the payment was too high and the rents would not cover it so I decided to just refinance it and consolidate the $5k credit card that was at 29% interest rate.

Mr. Reitz had agreed on a no prepayment penalty contract but when he submitted the paperwork to the bank for the payoff he charged me 3 points.

I argued about it but he said his time was valuable and that nobody does any kind of paperwork for free and flat out refused to accept anything less than what he had asked for, 3 points. He said it was not a prepayment penalty it was the cost for preparing the payoff paperwork. I could not win the fight and had to pay the additional fee, luckily I was able to add it to the loan.

I was so disappointed with him, he seemed like such a nice older man and now I felt like I was being ripped off but I was still happy that I was able to get out of the private loan and into a new one at a much lower interest rate. I was still confident, that with my high credit rating, credit limits and prosperous employment I could overcome anything that would come my way. I always think that there is always a solution to any problem!

THE AGONY AND ECSTASY
OF THE LANDLORD

In the 4th month of pleasure for having all leases signed and all running semi-smoothly in the middle of the month, Mr. and Mrs. Flores called me to tell me that they would be out of the house at the end of the month. The lady said a relative had been deported to Mexico and they had to move with that family to help out while the family member was out of the country and they didn't know for how long that would be, they just had no choice.

I knew I had a contract signed for 5 years but how could I enforce it or sue them to make them pay for the 5 years they had agreed to, they had nothing for me to go after. At this point I didn't even have the security deposit to hold on to. It was a good thing I had not given them the furniture and household goods I was still collecting from my house and family members to give to them. I had no choice but to let them go.

Luckily these tenants left the place clean, the yard had some plants and it looked better than when they first arrived. I was disappointed to see them leave but I needed to move on and find a new tenant.

When I began interviewing I found out that this is the trend of most of the farm workers; they move every few months following the crops and that is why they don't accumulate furniture, household goods or even much clothing. They are never stable anywhere, if they have kids the kids go to up to 4 or 5 different schools in one year, almost like gypsies. Now it all makes sense, unfortunately I did not know about this trend.

It took a while to find suitable tenants, very few Spanish-speaking people would apply, I still don't know why because there is a great deal of them in the area.

One day as soon as I got home from having an open house all day, with only a couple of shows, who took the application but were too busy to fill it out right there for me, I got a call from Mr. Reveles saying he had passed by the house, saw it and loved it and wanted to see the inside at that moment!

I told him I was not able to do that because I was 2 hours away, at least, but would be happy to show it to him the next day. He was disappointed and said that tomorrow would be too late; He was with his family and they needed a place to sleep that night.

Mr. Reveles, his wife and 3 little girls had been evicted and he had all their belongings in the back of his truck. I asked why they had been evicted and he said because he did not have a job and by the time they had the money together to catch up with the rent the landlord didn't want to take it and kicked them out. But he assured me he had a job now and the cash on hand for the first month and security deposit and was willing to fill out the application over the phone in order to be able to move in the house that night.

One of the windows had not been replaced with a new lock and a small person could get in with no problem I figured the kids could get in and let them settle for the night, just felt so bad knowing they had kids and no place to sleep.

I had a bad feeling about rushing into doing this but went ahead and took the application over the phone and told him to wait around there until I could verify employment and call the references etc. Luckily it was early enough for me to call in and verify employment and was able to contact the references right away.

Employment was verified and the three references told me how nice of a couple they were and how family oriented, hard workers and neat they were, nothing negative about them, of course!

The tenants were going to hang out at the house, outside under the porch in hopes I would call them to let them in the house and approve the lease. They were willing to sign a 5 or 10-year lease if I wanted. I told them we would do a 1-year lease for now and depending on how they liked it then we would renew for a longer term.

I called the tenant back and told him that one of the windows did not have a lock and if his kids were small enough they could go in and open the door for them. I told him I would have the application for them ready to sign in the morning, I would come up at 10 am and told him to have the cash on hand along with the rest of the documents I needed like his driver's license, and all.

Ah what a nice feeling, I am putting a roof over these poor unfortunate people, what a blessing to be a landlord, even thought I still didn't feel comfortable rushing like that and letting them in without me being there, not a good thing at all! I was risking them just staying there and not pay rent for 6 moths or more until I would evict them but how could I let these little ones sleep in the streets? They sounded so sincere and in such a need. I convinced myself it was a good thing and I was just being paranoid from my previous experience and prayed the next morning things would get sorted out.

When I arrived the next day, I woke them up. I peaked inside the house and the entrance was full of furniture, mattresses, kids on top of the mattresses, toys, etc. The tenant had gone to sleep late because he was busy bringing in the house all their belongings. The little girls looked like dolls and the couple looked like models. Young, beautiful and so thankful I let them in with such a short notice. Seeing all the stuff they had gave me a sort of reassurance that they were planning on being there for a long time and that was a good thing!

He gave me the cash right away, signed the lease, showed me his driver's license for me to take a picture of but said the wife's driver's license was somewhere in the pile of stuff, she was not sure where her purse was and as soon as she would find it they would send me a copy of it. He kept telling me over and over how super thankful they were for me trusting them and said they were hoping not to move from this place ever, they loved everything about the house!

The drive back home was nice, I had a month and a half of rent covered, this was the middle of September and the rent was pro-rated for the month. But most of all I was so happy that this nice family had a roof over their heads. What a blessing being a Landlord!

By this time, Mr. and Mrs. Otto, the newly married couple started to pay a few days late, she was giving me excuses of mailing the payment but it was mailed without a stamp, she was still not able to produce any income, she had to pay emergency vets visits for her cat, the husband had fewer days at work because of bad weather and he was not able to drive the truck, she had doctors visits related to her trying to get pregnant, etc... etc.. then they began to fall behind on the rent, they would pay me 30 or 40 or 50 % of the rent but would not let me know that they were short on the rent I would find out only after I would receive the rent in the mail, so I had to constantly be calling them to find out what was going on.

The house was looking neglected and every month there was something to fix, the toilet, the kitchen, the heater, the cooler, etc. They placed a lock on the gate because they got a big dog, without my permission. We had agreed they could keep one cat as pet and that was it. When I found out about the dog I told them they had to get rid of it because that was not in our agreement. They gave me a sad story and since I am a big dog lover I agreed for them to keep him. Next time I went to the house they had 2 big dogs and the yard was a mess! The front porch had the wood parts all chewed up from the dogs; all the plants outside were gone there was only dirt and holes from the dogs digging everywhere including by the posts where the porch was already tilting. I told them if they wanted to keep the dogs they had to clean, pick up after them, give me a dog deposit and replace the material things the dogs had damaged, which was a growing list!

And by now I was super busy at work. It was getting more and more difficult to deal with these far away properties. It was not easy to go as often as I wanted and sometimes go only to pay the handymen that most of the time only took cash as payment, it took so much time to show and interview prospect tenants and workers. I started to consider hiring a property manager.

I began interviewing property managers which were also very few to chose from. I ended up hiring one that Mr. Reitz had recommended before. She was a sweet older lady, Ms. Conte, who lived and was a property manager in town all her life and had a daughter, Mrs. Uresti who worked for her and also lived locally. Her fee was 6% and she had a handyman she trusted that took care of her rentals but would not manage the current tenants only the future ones if I wanted to, she was flexible and understanding. I felt I could trust her just by our first conversation over the phone, a nice gut feeling that I had not had in a long time! The fee was worth the time and money I was spending with the many trips. Feeling so comfortable with Ms. Conte I convinced her to manage all the tenants including the current ones and she agreed.

Very soon I realized how much less for rents I was receiving after paying the property manager and paying the handymen every time something needed to get fixed, which was at least one incident per property per month but it was still worth it for her to handle it in exchange for my time and efforts.

It was November 5st the first rent was due for the model couple, Mr. and Mrs. Reveles and I had not received it, it was actually due on the 1st but I give all tenants 5 additional days just in case it gets lost in the mail etc. If it is not received on the 5th then a late fee is applied. I had not heard anything from them since we signed the lease, I assumed all was going well and there was nothing to fix otherwise they would've called me already.

When I called to remind them that the rent had not been received, he told me that well, it was a sensitive subject because they were really not married, they were just boyfriend and girlfriend and they had broken up and he was no longer living there. He said to contact her and arrange payment. I reminded him that he had signed the one-year lease with her making them both responsible and technically both were liable for the entire year. He quickly had to hang up because he was at work and was not able to talk on the phone, he would definitely call me back as soon as he would get out of work but told me to call her and collect the money from her.

When I talked to her she apologized and said she was sorry but that she was expecting the welfare check and she had not received it, apparently it had been lost so they were re-issuing another one and she will send me the money as soon as she would receive it. After talking to her I let Ms. Conte handle it.

Ms. Conte told me that during this time of year most tenants don't pay because of the holidays coming up and they know landlords won't evict during the holidays. Needless to say I was surprised to hear that, never had I ever heard of such a thing!

When Ms. Conte tried contacting Mr. Reveles, his phone number was disconnected and he was nowhere to be found. The mother and the kids were in the house making up any excuse possible for not paying the rent. The house was a mess and they had people there all the time, all ages, it was a busy household.

November passed and December came and there was no rent from these folks. Ms. Conte gave them a 3-day notice, to their surprise, and then eviction was the next step. Ms. Conte told me that if we were going to evict the eviction day was most likely going to be December 25th, Christmas Day and asked me if I was willing to do it, I said yes being confident that this will not happen.

The rent did not come after the 3-day notice and they would not even open the house when Ms. Conte would go to collect it or to talk to them.

Sure enough they were evicted on Christmas day. Not such a good feeling to be a landlord that day.

Ms. Conte recommended I take Mr. Reveles, who was responsible for the lease to small courts for payment of the year lease. We filed in small claims court but the guy was never to be found to be served, he was no longer working at the place he was working when the lease was signed and most likely skipped town. We placed a lien on him but never got any kind of money or heard anything about him at all.

Needless to say, all these additional expenses kept on coming and my credit cards balances were growing by the minute. The Insurance and taxes payments came too quickly and of course I didn't have the cash to cover them but no problem, I had plenty of credit cards to pay the bills with and I charged them.

At this point I was getting disillusioned, I know it, I should've been 100% disillusioned already but I continued to be optimistic about the properties and hoping in time it would all work out for the best.

Ms. Conte found an older couple interested in renting the house but the rents had to be reduced a bit because they lived on social security and were not in the best of health to find employment. The house was perfect for them because it was small it was one story and was close enough for them to walk to the market and Laundromat.

Again, it was a good feeling to know I was helping out someone in need even if my monthly cash flow was not as high as I had initially expected but felt blessed to be able to do this, at this time.

Mr. Hazan who lived in one of the units decided to move back to his country. No worries I had a property manager now to handle these problems and together we would solve any problems.

We went from tenant to tenant and I stopped going to the properties, less and less, as long as the property manager was handling the problems and fixing them I gave her all the authority to make the necessary decisions.

The tenant problems never stopped. One tenant who lived in one of the properties was a single older gentleman with health issues and yes, limited income, we gave him many opportunities to catch up but the outstanding bill was getting higher and higher and he suggested to allow his girlfriend to move in with him so she could pay a portion of the rent which we agreed to and a few months after she moved in, they started getting behind again and again but we felt that since they did catch up the first time they would do so this time too. The gentleman went out of state to visit his daughter and due to his poor health the trip was too much for him and as soon as he got back to town, he passed away.

What do we do now? There was a pretty substantial outstanding balance due and if the girlfriend didn't pay we would have to evict.

It took about 6 months to evict her because her name was not in the contract and she fought all the way. She left owing all the money that was owed, her teenage son who was upset because his mother was evicted trashed the place as much as he could and told anyone that would listen to him how I was a slum lord and how badly they were treated and he wanted to make sure I would not take advantage of anyone else. When they finally left there were broken windows, the garage and the house full of trash and old furniture, etc.

The cost to repair the property was almost $2,000.00, which of course I had to charge and the outstanding balance due was over $3,000.00 plus the eviction costs.

Another of the units needed lots of repairs and one of the tenants recommended her friend and family as tenants, Mr. and Mrs. Rodriguez. They were contractors and they would fix the unit in lieu of the deposit and first month rent. We agreed immediately!

Mr. and Mrs. Rodriguez with their 3 little kids, 2 girls and 1 boy. They initially did a bit of work, which gave us hope that this will work out. Then the work stopped, they hid from us every time we went to the unit to talk to them; they disconnected their phone and changed their cell phone numbers; they had 2 dogs trashing the place; they installed a fence behind them taking space from the other tenants and they were not paying the utilities.

The other tenants found out their electricity and water bills were getting bigger and bigger every month. When the utility companies went to inspect the properties they found out Mr. and Mrs. Rodriguez had connected their house to the other tenants and they were stealing the electricity and water. When confronted by the police Mr. and Mrs. Rodriguez said I approved and actually recommended they should do that for the benefit of the kids.

When I told the officer that I never told the tenant to do so he asked me if I would press charges and I immediately said yes! Mrs. Rodriguez got on the phone begging me to say I did tell them because there was no way she could go to jail. All I said was; "You finally want to talk to me after I have been looking for you for so long, it is too late now." They took Mrs. Rodriguez to jail and they pressed charges for child endangerment as well. After she left jail they moved across county leaving the place like a pigsty.

Another great sweet older couple, were not in good health, very frail looking, had their disability payment as their only income and started getting behind every month after the first couple of months of moving in until one day she told me they could no longer afford to live there and the stairs were getting harder and harder for them to use. They would pay me back what was due as soon as they could gather the money if not right away then they would send me $200.00 monthly payments until it was paid off, they owed me over $2,000.00. The month passed and they were still there so we asked what was going on and she sent me a text saying: "We will leave in one more month and we are not paying anything else due, you do whatever you want to do".

Another tenant, single mother with 3 teenagers, who used to work as a waitress and got paid in cash had problems paying the rent on time because she used to hide the cash under the mattress or around the house, she did not have a bank account, and the kids would steal it from her and by the time the rent was due the money was almost gone or most of the time it was gone. She tried to pay in small payments and kept falling behind more and more every day. Then she thought things might get a bit better because her boyfriend was going to move in with her to help her out. And that is when she started falling more and more behind because the boyfriend would ask her for cash and she did not know how to say no to him. He didn't have a job and needed money to go to bars and for his smoking habits. Yes, another eviction! Along with an outstanding balance and many repairs to the house to be made.

By now Mr. and Mrs. Otto were still having problems catching up with the total due in rent, the house was being destroyed and because they were not willing to cooperate or negotiate with us we were going to be forced to evict them but one day Ms. Conte called to tell me the couple left the house keys with the neighbors and they were gone leaving the place a complete mess including the cat litter and a junk car which only cost me money to haul away.

Another great tenant, who moved in with his wife and two kids were solid renters, paid on time but always had problems with the kids toys being stuck in the toilet and our monthly plumbing bill started to grow until I told them they had to pay for the next plumbing bill. He was making decent money, he was the sole provider supporting the wife and 3 kids. He was an electrician and was working for a big company outside of town. As the economy started to turn he got laid off and began falling behind on the rent but because he had such a great paying record with us and we knew he was actively looking for work, we started letting him pay a little bit at a time. One day he flat out just asked us to reduce the rent because at the rate we were going he was never going to be able to catch up.

We reduced the rent not only to help them out but also because there were more and more vacant properties around and we knew they would bounce back once he was able to find a job. Since he did not have enough money from his unemployment to pay for the rent, support the family and make the truck payment, he felt behind on his truck payments and the truck was repossessed. Now he did not have the truck or any vehicle to look for a job. The wife started to work at a fast food place and he fell into a deep depression, started drinking and just did not care anymore and stopped trying. I could no longer carry them. Yes, again I got stuck with a pretty hefty outstanding balance.

There was a tenant with a 6 year-old daughter looking for a place to rent, he had just gotten divorced and had no place to go to with his daughter. He applied and employment was verified along with references etc. and they moved in. One month after they moved in he was laid off. Coincidence? I think not! He stopped paying the rent offering to pay only one third because he just had too much of a hard time finding a job and carrying for his 6 year old daughter.

We began the eviction process and he made us an offer of cash for keys to move out. I told him I would rather pay the eviction fee and after a few months he was finally evicted. He kept hiding from anyone serving him any legal papers and it took awhile to get rid of him. He left the house full of trash and lots of furniture; the garage was full of furniture, clothes, dishes, groceries, etc. as well as the outside balcony. The carpet was wet and full of mud; there were two broken windows, etc.

One day Mrs. Uresti called me to tell me Ms. Conte had passed away. I knew she was ill but didn't know to what extent. It was a very sad day; I never got to meet this lady whom I spoke with almost every day. Mrs. Uresti assured me everything was going to be the same, from now on she was going to handle all the accounts her mom had which she was doing anyway, but her mom was just the point of contact with the property owners.

I began to worry about Mrs. Uresti also leaving town since the passing of her mom and by now I understand that the properties are too far away for me to manage, as much as I hated to admit it and decided to continue with her services.

Since the passing of Ms. Conte the economy got worse and worse, the problems with the tenants continued one thing after another.

The beautiful old and enormous tree that was giving shade to the properties fell on one of the units, the bottom was rotten due to lack of water and the roof and part of the property structure was damaged and it had to get fixed quickly before the rain season.

The property values were below 70% of the purchase price and more and more I just did NOT want to deal with them anymore! I could not sell them without having a negative balance so I tried refinancing the loan with a lower interest rate but was not able to because of the low rents and negative monthly profits.

I tried modifying the loan with one of the government programs but was not able to do so due to my husband's high-level income. I attempted to just walk away from the properties but because we had a good amount of equity in our primary residence and other investments I was advised not to do it, the lender could go after any of our investments.

How is it possible that no decent tenants applied ever! The bill for Mr. Long, the handyman, kept growing and growing and the cash flow was less and less every month. I had not visited the properties in a few years and decided to take a trip there and meet with Mrs. Uresti. One of the units needed to be cleaned before renting it and I decided I was going to do it myself to save some money. I made an appointment with Mrs. Uresti to meet me there, she told me she had to go out of town and would not be able to meet me but I still went to see the properties and clean the one that needed to be rented out.

When I arrived at the unit I was shocked! I thought I was going to have a heart attack! All three properties looked like they had not been touched in years! There was no way I was going to be able to clean this particular unit by myself in one day, my heart just sank and right then I wondered where did all the money I had been paying to Mr. Long went? I called Mr. Long and when he came he told me that he had been the one repairing the properties and that there was an outstanding balance of over $500.00 that Mrs. Uresti said I would pay him! He was a very nice guy, he said his wife was the one doing the cleaning after each tenant left and they were happy to do it again for this new unit that needed to be cleaned. He told me they were also the crew who worked with Mrs. Uresti to clean and fix her own rentals in town. Apparently Mrs. Uresti owned over 20 units in town.

He told me that one of my flaky tenants was one that used to rent from Mrs. Uresti when Mrs. Uresti evicted her she placed her in my unit!

Now all of a sudden I started to suspect the integrity and motives of Mrs. Uresti and wondered if she was placing the quality tenants in her units instead of mine but I didn't say anything to her, I just made another appointment to meet. I wanted her to tell me face to face where and how all the money for repairs had gone. When we met she told me that with all the expenses and repairs she did not have enough money to pay Mr. Long and we had an outstanding bill with him of over $500.00 and another outstanding bill at the local hardware store for over $700.00. She also mentioned that she was busy looking for a place for one of the tenants we had evicted before from one of my properties. I asked her why was she doing that when she was the one that had evicted that tenant from my unit and she said: 'Oh that is how we do it here, I place them wherever I can'

Her response confirmed my doubts about her integrity and that was the last drop, I decided to sell these properties 'ASAP' even if I would end up upside down, I was already there! I was dry on my savings, all my credit cards were up to the limit and I had no rental income coming, I was running negative every month.

I felt defeated and a failure in every aspect, as an investor, as a property manager, as a wife, as a person, as a landlord, even as a friend! Sadly I had no more steam I was done at this point no more ecstasy being a landlord only agony.

INCOME, EXPENSES AND MORE

Because of the economy downfall turning worse and worse the credit card companies were also being more selective and strict on their lending practices. The commercial lenders were being more cautious with their lending and some completely stopped lending. This was without a doubt going to affect my income, which was mostly commission based on commercial lending.

The credit limit to my credit cards was reduced and the companies closed my credit cards that had zero balance because I did not use them. All of a sudden my credit score dropped to a number I had never had! While my credit balances were getting higher and higher, my credit rating was getting lower and lower.

Knowing that my job, as well as my husband's job could be in jeopardy and our household outstanding debts being at the level of our current salaries I began to worry more and more every day. My husband and I started looking at various businesses to buy, this was the time to do so, I always wanted to be an entrepreneur. Many of these businesses just wanted to break even and were selling at a very reasonable price.

After much research we found a business that fit our bill and one that could easily keep me employed at the same salary as I was used to, or even higher and it was something my husband was interested in, we were excited and made an offer, which was accepted right away!

I was going to turn in my resignation notice on a Monday and on the Friday before, the owner of the company announced that the company was closing down that day! Due to the nature of the business, being commissioned based and the confidentiality issues, there was no compensation for termination period, all employees were terminated and had to leave the premises that day. No worries, I was going to leave anyway and now I could concentrate on our business acquisition, which was already in escrow.

The day we were going to sign the closing documents for the business, the seller called and said he was not going to pay the agent his commission because he thought it was too much so he decided that at closing my husband and I should sign a document saying that if the agent would end up suing him for the commission, we would take the responsibility of dealing with it or we could just pay it at closing. Obviously we did not agree to those terms and cancelled escrow and the entire transaction, which ended up costing us a portion of the deposit.

At the same time we found out that our 9.5 year-old doggie had cancer and we had to operate immediately if we wanted to save her life. We ended up paying around $20k in vet bills and unfortunately we were not able to save her. Our hearts were broken, heavy and with so much remorse for not having noticed her illness sooner and maybe we could've saved her life. I blamed it on being so busy with the darn properties from hell that I neglected our precious doggie.

Now, the purchase of the business did not go thru, our puppy was gone, my job was gone, and the problems with the tenants from the properties from hell would not stop nor the credit charging to cover the expenses.

I fell into a deep depression; which didn't help the matters any and all of a sudden nothing mattered; I just wanted to watch TV to forget about all my problems.

Something needed to be done and soon, my expenses were by far exceeding the rents being collected and I had no other income. I used to wake up in the middle of the night turning and tossing wondering how I was going to get out of this situation. I tried to obtain a home equity line of credit on one of the properties that was paid off but my husband needed to sign the contract, since my husband did not know what I was going thru I didn't move forward with it because I did not want him to stress out over it and get his name involved it this mess. He was not too happy about me purchasing the properties to begin with; I was trying to handle it all by myself.

Job searching is never easy and mostly when the job requirements were as high as mine. I now needed a high paying job to cover my monthly expenses and also my husband's just in case his job was in jeopardy as well, with the economy going down and layoffs in his company happening I was in a constant state of fear. Sometimes I felt like I could not even breathe not knowing where or when my next paycheck would come.

Not many companies were hiring in my recent line of expertise, on the contrary, the companies were closing down, the jobs were getting fewer and fewer and the pool of candidates kept growing and growing. I even applied to opportunities in the Information Systems field where my expertise was outdated but those were the only jobs with salaries that would cover my expenses. I lost count of how many resumes I submitted, how many interviews I went to and how many phone calls I made unsuccessfully.

Then I focused on searching for businesses to purchase; I thought that was my only option to make the kind of money I needed to cover my expenses and possibly grow to cover my husband's salary if needed I am a hard worker with a great work ethic and welcome any challenges. I looked into all the industries, in any kind of industry that I could buy and manage only to annoy my husband. It really bothered him that I was not focused and was all over the place! Yes, I was all over the place trying to find a way out of the mess I was in and he had no idea how deep!

In order to make my monthly payments without an income I had to sell some of my jewelry, I did some online selling, recycling, used all my birthday and any cash gifts towards my debts, by now my husband was paying for all the things I used to pay for and he started to notice how much more of his income is going towards my debts so he was not happy. I tried to economize in every which way possible with coupons, no luxuries of any kind, cooking, washing and ironing instead of dry cleaning, skipping haircuts, etc. but it was just not enough, and at the same time trying to keep a happy face so my husband would not freak out if he knew my situation.

At my yearly physical exam, an MRI was suggested in addition to the mammogram because of the breast cancer running in my family.

The next day I got a call from the breast cancer center asking me to go back for a biopsy because something was detected in the new mammograms, they just wanted to rule out anything being malignant. The spots detected were so small that the biopsy had to be done twice, they kept missing the tiny spots but never the less it was done, quite painful but was done! They were going to get back to me with the results in a week or so but they were confident it was just a scare nothing to worry about.

The next day at 6:30 PM my primary doctor called me to tell me he didn't have good news, I was diagnosed with DCIS – Ductal Carcinoma In Situ, a very early stage of breast cancer, pre-cancerous cells were being developed and I needed to go thru the removal of them.

I had a lumpectomy done and fortunately the only treatment needed was a daily pill for 5 years, all the doctors said it was the earliest stage of cancer that can be found and felt I was very fortunate.

Needless to say, this event changed my world, all of a sudden I realized that if anything would happen to me my husband would be stuck with the mess of the properties from hell and all the credit card mess he had no idea of, I needed to do something right away. I always thought selling the properties would cover paying them off and the credit incurred because of them but I did not think of the economy turning around as bad as it did and now I had to deal with it the best way I could.

I decided to reinvent myself and obtain my loan originator license and work hard to get some income, any income even if it was not the one I was looking for eventually it would get there and actively started looking at how to get rid of these properties that I believed contributed to my health issues.

SAVING GRACE

I immediately began listing the properties for sale AS-IS even if they were upside down in value and state. Any offer would be considered!

Because of the condition they were in they did not meet the qualification for a traditional mortgage loan and the existing loan was not assumable. The only way I saw out of this was to do the loan myself with a private contract

I met with various investors interested but their offers were way below any acceptable amount, they wanted them almost free and I could not afford to pay the outstanding balances so I held on to them for as long as possible. Some of the investors wanted to buy just one property, some wanted to buy only two, etc. some would not even call me back after seeing the condition of the units.

It was a rollercoaster ride, I would promise an offer then the offer would never come, I would promise a follow up call and the call would never come, etc. I was getting more and more discouraged as time went by and worried about the liability with squatters in the empty units.

Two of the units were occupied but in one the tenants were in and out I had no more money to spend on evictions. As soon as they found out I was going to sell them, they decided to completely stop paying and wait for the new owners to evict them.

There was an ad in the local town's paper about another property being sold, financed by the owner and this house was in the same block as my properties.

I did some research and found out he was a handyman that fixed and flipped homes locally. I contacted him and asked him why he was not renting it instead of selling it. I just wanted to know more about the renting situation in the town, I still wanted to give Mrs. Uresti the benefit of the doubt and felt bad about not trusting her anymore and maybe renting them back was my only way out.

The seller of the property, Mr. Stroud went on to tell me that he was thinking about renting it instead of selling because they had other rental units and they were all very successful. His wife was the property manager and was tough with the tenants and they had no problems so most likely he will end up renting this place too. I asked him if he would be interested in buying my properties with minimum down payment and at a very reasonable rate with a note that I was willing to carry myself and I would work with them on the terms all the way. He sounded interested but said he needed to speak with his wife and they would call me back.

A few days passed and they didn't call. I assumed they went to see the houses and were scared with the state of them all, like the rest of the investors. I had two other investors interested but their terms were different than mine and we could not agree on a few things so I decided to call Mr. Stroud again and maybe I could speak with his wife and explain the situation myself.

When I called Mr. Stroud he said he and his wife were walking the dogs and would call me as soon as they would get home. Oh dogs, we have one more thing in common I thought!

Sure enough Mrs. Stroud called me back and told me how successful she was with their rental units, most of them were Spanish speaking tenants who worked in the local farming fields and had a month to month lease due to the nature of the job, the tenants were gone and back on a rotating basis yearly so their income was pretty steady.

Whoa! She was doing just what I had always wanted to do and it was possible I just did not know how to do it. She was the ideal person to purchase my properties and take over. She asked me of my situation and I was completely honest with her and told all about the properties and my experience with the property management, how my husband didn't even know about all the stress I was going thru including avoiding making calls in front of him about all my issues etc. I did not want to add any of my stress to whatever he was dealing with, I was almost in tears! She felt my sadness, my frustration and feeling of complete failure then she said; "Natasha, let me discuss your proposition with my husband, we need to go see the properties and prepare a very comprehensive estimate of what we would be getting into and will get back to you by tomorrow night.

She continue to say what I still remember word by word; "Natasha I am so sorry for you, I do not like it when people are being taken advantage of, would you be open to saying a prayer right now for you?" I felt my tears rolling down my cheeks, someone knew just how I felt, this was the first time I had confided in someone at this level about these properties from hell! And we, well she, said the most beautiful prayer which immediately gave me a sense of peace, hope, relief and some assurance that it was all going to be ok from now on.

The next day she called me and we arranged to meet. They were going to partner up with one more person, Mr. Jones who had inherited quite a bit of money and they were going to purchase them! Mr. Jones was going to live in the single unit and the couple was going to manage the duplex.

We met with their financial advisor and agreed on a selling price and terms and right now they are in the process of fixing the units, they have evicted the other tenants and I know they will make these the best rental units in the area, just like what they were supposed to be long time ago when I bought them. I am now carrying the note until they can refinance them or Mr. Jones receives his full inheritance and can pay them off. They make their payment early every month and I am able to stay current on my debts, which keep on declining a little bit at a time.

Thank the Lord, I can see the light at the end of the tunnel!

THE INEVITABLE

I never thought of the many things that can happen and are beyond our control. I was blinded by the excitement of being a landlord and the possibility of helping others.

Building wealth and financial freedom was my primary motivation to acquire as many properties as possible but never occurred to me that so many incidents can affect the outcome of our plans; we cannot be in control at all times but the more prepared we are the more we are able to deal with and handle the unexpected and inevitable situations such as all that I experienced;

- Illness
- Job Loss
- Loss of Equity
- Economy

- Emergency expenses
- Being in debt
- Not being proactive
- Financial mistakes
- Not doing enough research about what we are getting into
- Accidents
- Mother nature
- Rushing into things and not being patient
- Not listening to our partner and/or family members advise

Looking back I believe I also lacked humility and had too much pride to ask for help. I know my husband would've done all things possible to relieve me from so much pain and stress that inevitably affected our relationship and our finances.

Rental properties never work out the way they are supposed to, one must have plenty of cash flow and never bent the rules to prevent them from eating us alive.

RECOMMENDED READINGS

The Total Money Makeover and Complete Guide to Money – Dave Ramsey.

ABOUT THE AUTHOR

Natasha Re resides in Simi Valley, California with her husband and two dogs.